I0116228

INSTANT REAL ESTATE INVESTOR BLUEPRINT

THE STEP-BY-STEP GUIDE TO INVESTING IN REAL ESTATE WITHOUT USING YOUR OWN CASH OR CREDIT

SMART
Real Estate
COACH

© Copyright 2020, Smart Real Estate Coach

All rights reserved.

This book may not be reproduced in whole or in part without written permission from the publisher, except by a reviewer who may quote brief passages in a review; nor may any part of this book be reproduced, stored in a retrieval system, or transmitted in any form or by any means, electronic, mechanical, photocopying, recording, or other, without written permission from the publisher.

Requests for permission should be made to:
support@smartrealestatecoach.com

Published by Wicked Smart Books
www.WickedSmartBooks.com

ISBN: 978-0-578-68206-8

Printed in The United States of America

This publication is designed to provide accurate and authoritative information in regard to the subject matter covered. It is sold with the understanding that the publisher is not engaged in rendering legal, accounting, or other professional services. If legal advice or other expert assistance is required, the services of a competent professional person should be sought.

DISCLAIMER

Please note that Chew Publishing, Inc. DBA/ SmartRealEstateCoach.com earnings are in no way average and that any examples provided should not be considered typical as your results will vary on many factors. Our team has been working in this niche for many years. If you think you can get rich by simply clicking a button or allowing others to do all the work, then we recommend you do not invest your money in any educational program or business tools as it will not be a good investment. Our team is here to support you and we hope that you make buying decisions because you are also dedicated to success.

From time to time, we send emails promoting other company's products or services and may earn commission for doing so. It is important to realize that while we only send products that we believe will help your business, we do not recommend investing into anything without doing you own due diligence. Like with anything in life, in order to succeed, you will need to put forth effort and be persistent. And finally, any information provided is education and cannot be taken as legal or financial advice.

We are not attorneys. Laws change in every State from time to time. Always check with your attorney before buying and/or selling real estate for the applicable laws in your area. These laws may or may not affect some of the techniques we teach. There are no laws to our knowledge that can STOP you from profiting in real estate, but you'll need to seek a qualified local real estate attorney.

As of the posting of this disclosure, we are aware of laws in the following areas that are different from most other states. If you are outside of the United States, your laws will vary and we are not familiar with them. This is not all inclusive and only those that we are aware of:

- Texas: Lease/purchase restrictions unless you comply with local changes.
- Maryland: Foreclosure laws within 20 days of foreclosure. We don't teach foreclosure. Some restrictions buying subject to existing mortgages.
- North Carolina: Comply with 3-day right of rescission as well as recording agreements when doing lease/purchase.
- California: Foreclosure property laws. We don't teach foreclosure.
- Florida: Licensing laws for lease purchase if you have a Seller Specialist working for you acquiring properties.
- Illinois: Assignment restrictions for wholesaling and AO deals.

CONTENTS

INTRODUCTION

When you're done with this book, our goal is to have you put your first home under agreement within 30-180 days. We have the benefit of working with some amazing students all over North America and what is super clear now is that your time frame to your first deal is much more a result of your mindset and the mental side of your business versus any skill sets you can learn. We teach the same thing to all of our students, yet they all produce their first deal in different time frames.

Our main foundational home study course, The Quantum Leap Systems Home Study Program (otherwise referred to as QLS), gives you literally all that you need on the real estate side of things. On the mental side of the business, we've partnered with Dr. Joe Vitale (70+ time best-selling author, one of the amazing members who filmed The Secret, and Smart Real Estate Coach's Keynote speaker at our QLS Live event in 2018) to create The 31-Day Billionaire course.

You can learn more about either of these courses by visiting:
smartrealestatecoach.com/qls, and
smartrealestatecoach.com/billionaire

SMART REAL ESTATE COACH'S PURPOSE
To empower individuals and families to create the life of their dreams.

SMART REAL ESTATE COACH'S CORE VALUES
- We constantly innovate and improve
- We complete all transactions with the highest integrity
- We match effort for effort
- We are clear, blunt, and to the point — no gray area
- Team over ME

Let's get started.

I'm going to be explaining different options you have within the Sandwich Lease technique – one of many techniques we use to buy and sell properties. For a full explanation of our business, you can get one of our best-selling books on Amazon, *Real Estate on Your Terms* or *The New Rules of Real Estate Investing*. Keep in mind that we buy and sell as a family company in Massachusetts, Rhode Island, and Connecticut primarily. So, although this works anywhere, some of the legal and technical things may change in your state. We coach, mentor, and do deals with students in several different states, as well as Canada.

NOTE: *IF YOU ARE IN THE STATE OF TEXAS, DO NOT THINK YOU CANNOT DO LEASE/OPTIONS. YOU CAN BUY ON TERMS OR LEASE/PURCHASE AND YOU CAN SELL ON TERMS OR ASSIGN YOUR LEASE/OPTION. GET YOURSELF INTO OUR ASSOCIATE PROGRAM SO WE CAN GET THAT GOING WITH YOU.*

To avoid referencing the Resource section in the back of the book continuously, just know that everything I mention for resources, tools or contacts can be found in that section. This alone is worth thousands of dollars, even if we never have a chance to meet.

Our QLS Home Study Program mentioned above has all of our training materials, resources, and more for you. We update it continuously and it's online at our Smart Real Estate Coach Academy (**smartrealestatecoachacademy.com**) for your continued access.

NOTE: *All QLS Home Study Program purchases include one (1) ticket to our QLS Live Event held each year here in Rhode Island.*

WHAT ARE "SANDWICH LEASES"?

You might be wondering what I mean when I say "sandwich lease." A Sandwich Lease is created when you put a home under agreement via a lease/purchase document and then turn around and sell the home via lease/purchase (the market statistically searches by and understands "Rent to Own," but it's the same thing) to your buyer. By doing that, you'll create a Payday #1 when you secure your buyer, and accept a nonrefundable deposit, a Payday #2 will accrue monthly as they pay their lease and you keep the difference between that and your payment out to either the Seller or their bank, and a nice juicy Payday #3 on what I call the back end, which is when your buyer gets financing and cashes you out.

You will have the option (and in Texas, a must) to assign the contract back to your seller and only have Payday #1 -- *but more on that later*. Our average Payday #1 "Assignment Fee" (we call those deals 'AO' meaning Assign Out in Texas or anywhere you do these) as of this writing is just under $28,000. How many of those Paydays do you need monthly? All 3 Paydays average us right now approximately $75,000. For all of our Associates around North America, the averages are between a low of $45,000 and a high of $200,000.

The 3 Paydays is our ideal setup, but sometimes if you don't see a monthly and/or back end possibility (we teach you how to determine that in our **QLS Home Study Program**, of course) the deal can still be very lucrative with just Payday #1 by simply procuring your tenant/buyer, assigning them back to the seller, and keeping a nice assignment fee. Our average in 2014 was $10,800, in 2015 approached $15,000, and our average this year is approaching $28,000 as we get smarter and smarter over time!

Think about what I just shared with you – we show you how to do your own Sandwich Lease deals and you average $10k-$30k per deal if assigning back (AO) or $45,000-$200,000 per deal if you complete all 3 Paydays. *Hmm, how many of those do you need monthly?* At the time of this writing, we do a few per month and another 10-15 monthly (and growing) with students around the country through our revenue sharing Associate Levels. For more on that, check out our free webinar anytime at **smartrealestatecoach.com/webinar**

SELLER SCENARIOS

Why would a seller sell to you via Lease/Purchase and not just sell the property outright? There are several reasons that I've seen in doing these, but here are a few along with the structure you would use.

Keep in mind that, as you do these, you will have equitable interest in the home protected by a Notice of Option recorded on the property and you'll do so with NONE of your own funds. Let's look at some scenarios:

- **SCENARIO #1: SELLER OWES MORE THAN THE PROPERTY IS WORTH**

  Long term lease/purchase whereby the principal reduces and the market increases over time for you. The seller is thrilled to have mortgage taken care of.

- **SCENARIO #2: SELLER OWES ABOUT WHAT IT IS WORTH SO, IF THEY GO TO THE CLOSING TABLE, THEY WOULD LIKELY HAVE TO COME UP WITH CASH THAT THEY DON'T HAVE OR DON'T WANT TO PART WITH**

  We do a lot of these, as long as we can see a monthly spread. There's a nice principal reduction over time and enough room to capture our premium price. It's the same as the over-leveraged example above, but the term doesn't have to be quite as long. You can determine how long by checking the approximate principal pay down monthly on the mortgage and then just calculate how many years you'll need based on the profit you want to create on the back end. I personally don't do Sandwich Lease deals unless the total profit exceeds $50,000 counting all 3 Paydays, but you will make your own decisions.

- **SCENARIO #3: SELLER HAS TRIED TO SELL FSBO (FOR SALE BY OWNER) OR WITH A REAL ESTATE AGENT AND, FOR ANY NUMBER OF REASONS, HAS NOT HAD SUCCESS.**

Our virtual assistant calls all of our FSBOs and sends us completed property information sheets (nowadays they are loaded directly to our CRM or our Associates' CRM). You can find contact information for virtual assistant services on the Investor Resources section of our website: **smartrealestatecoach.com/resources**

Our Associates have access to our private team of Virtual Assistants and that cuts down on costs, set-up time, and, as a result, TTFD (time to first deal). Our private team of Virtual Assistants is continuously trained by us on a weekly basis.

Our #2 deal source is Expired Listings (homes that were with a real estate agent and didn't sell) and are a great lead source because they're already frustrated. Many have already formed a less-than-positive opinion about their real estate agent or agents in general (I know this because I was an agent and broker/owner for over 18 years). These sellers tend to be faster to act than a FSBO – because many, if not all, FSBO sellers clearly think they can sell on their own. As a result, sometimes FSBOS simply take more time and follow-up.

- **SCENARIO #4: SELLER HAS NO DEBT ON THE HOME, JUST WANTS TOP DOLLAR, AND DOESN'T MIND WAITING TO GET THAT**

This goes for any of the other scenarios as well. We've done many properties that were 100% debt-free and they were over $500,000 homes. These are nice because you can do owner financing with terms (a different book and different seminar!) as well as the Sandwich Lease Option.

I have to say, even though this book is focused on lease/options, my favorite strategy by far is owner financing with 100% principal payments monthly. You can learn more in our best-selling book **Real Estate On Your Terms** or enjoy Module 7 in the **QLS Home Study Program**.

- **SCENARIO #5: BURNT-OUT LANDLORDS ARE ALWAYS A GREAT SOURCE.**
  (SEE EXAMPLE 58W LATER IN THIS BOOK)

The FRBO (For Rent By Owner) would be about the same amount of deals as Expired Listings, but let's call that our #3 deal source. It's a long term lease/purchase whereby the principal reduces and the market increases over time for you. The seller is also thrilled to have the mortgage taken care of.

To be clear about how these virtual assistants are being most efficient, they are not spending time looking ("sourcing") these FSBO, Expired Listings, and FRBOs. They use our lead generation tool, My +Plus Leads, which can be found in the Investor Resources section on our website.

BUYER SCENARIOS

Why would a buyer want to acquire a home via Lease/Purchase instead of getting a conventional mortgage? I could write a book just on the stories we've heard from buyers and we absolutely love helping them get into homes and solving their challenges, but here are just a few to give you an idea of who your market is as well as some specifics that we've worked with.

By the way, if you are one of our Associates, you have 100% access to all the videos you see for buyers and sellers on our website, private labeled and ready to use. You can apply for one of our Associate Level Programs on our website. Associates also have the added credibility of a letter we send them to submit to their local BBB (Better Business Bureau) as well as feature them on our national website: **nationalpropertyteam.com**.

I hope you're getting the point that we equip our Wicked Smart Community with amazing tools, support, and more so that they can do deals – and do them more quickly for more profit. They love hanging out and helping each other on our private Slack channel as well.

- **SCENARIO #1: CREDIT CHALLENGES**

    Many things cause this, but those buyers that don't have a long-term challenge with this (in other words, a life event happened rather than poor habits or poor discipline) are some of the best and also the fastest to fix.
    - Death
    - Identity theft
    - Spouse abusing credit
    - Family member abusing credit via consignor or other
    - Bankruptcy
    - Foreclosure

- **SCENARIO #2: SEASONING**

Sometimes banks want to see more time on a job if a buyer is moving to another state or changing a job/profession. Some of these buyers are the best because it's not a credit issue; many of them have great credit and just need time. We recently had a landscaper move to RI from NY and needed seasoning, as well as two young buyers that were finishing law school and needed the same thing. The latter put down over $30,000 on a home that we assigned back to the owner and gladly collected a $15,000 assignment fee.

We now keep 25%-50% of the deposits when assigning back, but that came over time and is one of the many videos you'll see us cover on our free YouTube channel (**youtube.com/smartrealestatecoach** – *be sure to subscribe!)*. We release 3 videos every week for you: Deal Structure Sundays, Motivational Mondays, and Q&A Thursdays.

- **SCENARIO #3: THEY DISLIKE BANKS – *PERIOD.***

Don't we all!?

REAL SANDWICHES

Let's review just a few deals that we have done to give you a sense of where the deal came from, the supporting facts, built-in lessons, and the profits involved. We'll alter the real address for privacy reasons. Many more deals like this are broken down for you on our weekly Deal Structure Sunday videos on YouTube.

EXAMPLE #1: SINGLE FAMILY, 15 U, RHODE ISLAND

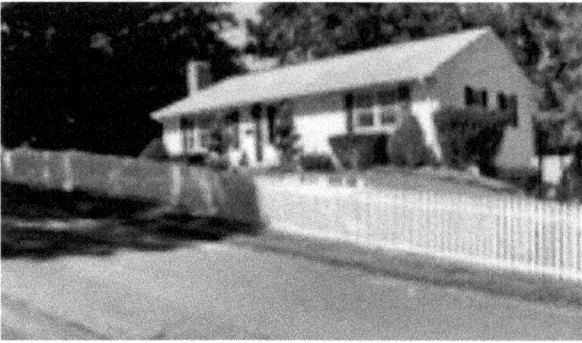

This lead came from an expired listing call that I made personally (now most of our calls and leads are generated by our virtual assistant, but our team still occasionally dials. It keeps us on the pulse, we enjoy it, and heck, what else is there to do when everything is automated?). As of this writing, my participation in the day-to-day business is minimal now that the VA's and our family team generate all the business and have taken over all buying and selling.

I met with the seller and found out she owed approximately $170,000 with a monthly payment including PITI (principal, interest, taxes, and insurance all-in-one payment) of approximately $1,290. The market at the time did not bring her the asking price of $185,000. Her goal was to sell, pay the commission and expenses, and move to another state. We structured a lease/purchase for no money down (always) and a purchase price at the end of 48 months of the exact mortgage balance remaining. We calculated that balance to be reducing at the rate of approximately $400/month. So, after 48 months, the balance remaining will be approximately $150,800.

EXIT: SOLD ON A LEASE TO OWN FOR $199,900 WITH $15,000 DOWN AND $1,600/MONTH. Remember the 3 Paydays I mentioned earlier?

- Payday #1: $15,000 down
- Payday #2: $310/month
- Payday #3: Approximately $34,000

LET'S REVIEW: $15,000 + $14,800 ($310 x 48 months) + $34,000 = **$63,800**

This deal had a very interesting twist and it will highlight another more advanced strategy that we love - converting Sandwich Leases to Subject To (existing loan) purchases. The couple in the home broke up prior to cash out and the gentleman stayed in the home. His time to purchase came and went. He wanted to simply stay and rent until he is mortgage ready. I called the seller and offered her $2,500 to deed the home over to me. She did. We still own the home and, as of this writing, the mortgage is only $113,000 while the value is approximately $265,000.

Converting a Sandwich to a Sub To versus trying to start out with a seller as a Sub To right away is easier because you've established some history, rapport, and trust by paying the mortgage over a period of months or years. We do several of these yearly.

The Paydays are nice, but think about the seller we helped move along to Florida and enjoy herself without worrying about her mortgage that, by the way, stays in her name until it's cashed out. Think also about the buyers who we helped who had almost given up on the home ownership dream and thought there was no answer for them. He's still in credit repair.

We now have the deed on this home and, frankly, don't care how long the buyer takes to get financing because now we have the benefit of longer term principal pay down. He has improved the home, built a nice fence around the property, and is definitely staying long term. He'll let me know if he gets financing but, in the meantime, he's paying off our home! Our back end Payday #3 just grew dramatically!

EXAMPLE #2: SINGLE FAMILY, 746 W, MASSACHUSETTS

This lead came from our VA and it was a FSBO. I met with the seller and found out he was not stressed at all and did not owe anything on the home which was worth approximately $900,000. Clearly he did not need me in the middle (meaning staying in the sandwich lease), so we openly discussed us simply finding the tenant/buyer and assigning this back to him (AO) for an assignment fee. When I was newer to TERMS deals, the AO was more prevalent in our business because it's simple. The huge disadvantage, of course, is there's only 1 Payday, so it feels more like a job. You'll hear me on our podcast often chat with guests about the 1 Payday nature of wholesale deals or rehab deals opposed to our deals which are mostly the 3 Paydays.

With this one, we found a tenant/buyer, got them prescreened, and arranged a $40,000 down payment. Our assignment fee for all this hard work is $22,500. In hindsight, we could have and should have negotiated a higher one (we do now, as I mentioned above) with the seller, but he's already referred us to others so we're okay with the $22,500 assignment fee.

EXAMPLE #3: TWO FAMILY, 58 W, MASSACHUSETTS

This was a FSBO. He is an accountant who used to live in the property. When the seller moved out with his family, he rented it out and ended up with nightmare tenants (one of the many reasons I don't do rentals – rent to own with skin in the game only). I tied up for the balance of the mortgage at the end of 9 years. I want you to think about that; up to 9 years to close it out with principal of approximately $325/month paying down (and growing monthly but for the math I'll use that as a fixed monthly amount so the profit will be conservative and lower than actual) on a $1340 per month payment. The balance when I started was $172,000. I sold it for $220,000 to a nice couple who live in one unit and they placed their parents and grandparents in the other unit. So, they have the entire property for $1950 – a $610 monthly net cash.

The two-family is an interesting one within this strategy because you can run it as a regular rental if you want to, short term, then convert to rent to own. I just don't like the headaches of regular rentals. We do on occasion just leave our properties as rentals and when we do we use a local management company, even on single families.

WHERE DO YOU FIND PROPERTIES?

As in any business, you must bring in leads. Lead generation is the lifeline to any business in any industry. I gave you a few links before to our Investor Resources page. Listed below are some typical seller sources. So, how do you get to those? You can totally automate this step in the process by having a virtual assistant make your calls for you. Our VA emails us (or loads in our CRM) on average 10-15 leads per week and we generate another 10-15 in-house. When you work with us, we will define EXACTLY how many leads you need weekly to convert to your financial goals and overall business plan.

Just to give you a taste of how that works: it takes on average 30-35 leads to get a check (10 to get an appointment and 17 to get a contract; yup, we know our numbers!) Let's take a look at where we get our leads here (you'll also want to go and download the special FREE "Get Deals Now" report for a complete lead generation report. Visit **smartrealestatecoach.com/report**).

- VA Calling Expired Listings
- VA Calling FSBOS
- Me or our team calling Expired Listings
- Me or our team calling FSBOS
- Field agents finding FSBO signs for you
- Family or Friends locating FSBO signs
  How about you give them $10 for every FSBO picture they send you?
- Yellow letter mailings to targeted lists
- Drive-bys

Your VA can source the FSBOs or you can source them and send the information to your VA to call. In addition to the resources you'll see listed in the back of this book and in the Special Report for lead generation, you can personally recognize properties in your area by taking different routes while driving each day instead of the same roads or highways. What can you look for? You can look for FSBO signs, run down properties, properties with handicap ramps (build a relationship for future sale with a handwritten note, yellow letter, or formal letter) and even land – but that's another course and another discussion! If you have not gone through our **Land: The Hidden Profit Center** Home Study Course, you're missing out on more profits – contact us for more information on that course!

GOOD LEADS VS. TOTAL DUDS

When a seller lead comes in, how do you identify whether it's a good lead or a total dud? To know this, you simply use the basic Property Information Sheet that I've been using for years. We've customized this sheet a few times to flow nicely with the conversation you have with the sellers. Not only does the form have the info you need, but it also has some scripting right on it.

The difference between a strong lead and a dud will be determined by these facts and, until you have these, you just don't know:

- What is their asking price?
- What do they think it is worth?
  (I'll often say in a conversational way: "What do you think it would appraise for?" or "I'm curious, did you have it appraised or did a real estate agent give you that number or how did you come up with that?" This usually gets them talking.)
- How much do they owe on it?
- What is the monthly payment and does it include PITI?
- Are they current on their payments?
- Why are they selling?
  (Again, this is a good open-ended question that gets them talking and one of the most important variables we looked at. We are in the business of solving challenges, solving problems, and offering great solutions. Find out WHY first and foremost, then provide the solution.)
- Any major repairs needed?

Keep in mind that you and/or your virtual assistant will be doing these calls. At this point in my business, as I mentioned above, my family/kids and a team run almost all of the buying and selling of our properties. I do calls for our team to stay on top of it, but just a few a day. I do most of my calling for and with my High 6 Associates' deals.

DEAL STRUCTURING

Okay, now you have a lead sheet and need to structure an offer that is profitable for both you and the seller. This is where the fun starts! These sellers are going to be in one of four buckets, as I refer to them. You can learn more about "buckets" in our book **Real Estate on Your Terms**. The four buckets are:

1. Property is Free & Clear – no mortgages or liens.
2. Property has a mortgage or two but still plenty of equity.
3. Property has a mortgage with just a little equity.
4. Over leveraged.

There are obviously more scenarios, but these will get you started in your journey of learning TERMS. You can turn any one of those buckets into a deal once you understand how to construct the right offer. Obviously, when you work in one of our Associate Levels, you will be structuring these alongside myself and my team, so your learning curve will be dramatically shortened!

On the property information sheet, one of the questions is whether or not they'll take payments on their equity or do a lease/purchase with you. If they want some large down payment that seems too high for you, you can still do the deal using the simple assignment option and if they'll take little money down and accept a low down payment, you can structure a nice owner financing deal.

For the sake of this book, we're going to stay with the lease/purchase or simple assignment option – but I cannot resist giving you two examples that I did with the same owner with properties side-by-side. Incidentally, this deal came to me while training a student and giving them some of my leads to call. He called, got the appointment, sat with me to structure the offers, and then met with the seller and wrapped the deal up for us.

The seller owned these two and wanted to retire to a different state. One home had no debt and one was over-leveraged. The one with no debt we structured a purchase price of $165,000 with no money down and monthly principal only payments of $850 and actually took title to the property – we now own it. We turned around and installed a great tenant/buyer with $8,000 down (remember, we didn't put any down, but paid the sellers' closing costs. So we spent approximately $1,800 leaving $6,200 net Payday #1) and $1,250 in monthly lease payments which became a nice spread for Payday #2 of $400. The sales price is $183,000. We have a five year balloon due on the mortgage, so we structured a 48 month lease purchase. Let's review this one:

- **PAYDAY #1:** $6,200 net
  (We literally never go this low now. All of our deals get to the 10% mark up front or over time, which not only improves our Payday #1, but also puts the buyer in a better position for their financing).
- **PAYDAY #2:** $400 x 48 months = $19,200
- **PAYDAY #3:** $50,800 ($165,000 less $40,800 paid at $850/month for 48 months is my payoff of $124,200. Sell price of $183,000 less $8,000 paid – so $175,000 due – net $50,800)

A nice total of the **3 PAYDAYS OF $76,200** primarily driven by the aggressive principal only pay down.

The 2nd home he had next door was structured as a typical lease purchase. He had a mortgage on it that was higher than what we were willing to pay. Therefore, we basically said we'll take the price we agreed upon of $145,000 and we'll chart the monthly principal paydown of the mortgage he's paying (he's paying more than I'm paying him monthly, which is only $800) which is approximately $300/month and that will be my credit off of the $145,000. This was structured with like the one he had next door, so we installed a tenant buyer for $1,250 monthly and a sales price of $155,000 with $5,000 down for 48 months.

- **PAYDAY #1:** $5,000
- **PAYDAY #2:** $450/month for 48 months = $21,600
- **PAYDAY #3:** $19,400 (I owe the seller $145,000 less $300 monthly principal paydown, which makes it $130,600. The buyer owes me $155,000 less $5,000 deposit, so $150,000)

TOTAL OF MY 3 PAYDAYS = $ 46,000

Let's play out the scenario of the first property we did with owner financing if the seller had said to me – I want $1200/month and I want a few thousand down with a selling price of $180,000.

What could I have done? I could simply put it under agreement with the understanding that there's not enough monthly spread or back end equity, so I would simply assign the buyer back to him and collect an assignment fee. The reason that would not have worked for him is because, remember, he was leaving the state and did not want to deal with it. When you let the seller speak and fill out the property sheet (or your VA does), you find out things like this that will help you know how best to structure the deal.

Let's transition now to bucket #2 – houses with a mortgage but plenty of equity. I'm working on one at the time of this writing that I intend to put under agreement this week, so I'll use that for the example.

This home is in Massachusetts and came to me via a fully filled-out property sheet from my VA. The seller was a FSBO and asking $325,900. My comps show a range of $335,000-$355,000, so I'll probably go on the market at $365,000. She owes approximately $75,000 on it, is a Doctor, lives a few hours away from this property in New York, and doesn't want to worry about it or deal with tenants. My offer to her is $1,500/month with a $300 credit to principal (I gave her $325,900) and a 48 month cash-out date. I'll sell for $365,000, $2000 monthly, and a 36 month term.

My projected Paydays are:

- **PAYDAY #1:** $36,000 down (we'll see – maybe more!)
- **PAYDAY #2:** $18,000 ($500/month spread for 36 months – more if it goes closer to 48 months)
- **PAYDAY #3:** $29,900 ($325,900 less my monthly credits of $300 x 36 months – $10,800 – so, I owe $315,100 and the buyer will owe $345,000).

Again, these are projections only, but those 3 Paydays = $83,900.

Now let's look at bucket #3 – property has a mortgage and just a little equity. For the sake of simplicity, I won't give you all the math on this one, but this is quite common and we have done many of these during the last 12 months.

By the way, speaking of 12 months – one of the really cool things about this TERMS model is that you get to take a break – get off the proverbial treadmill if you want, or ramp up and keep doing deals.

PROVEN SYSTEM
LAST 12 MONTHS: $ CREATED

$593,132.60 ⟫	$6,459.08 ⟫	$822,958.06 ⟫	**$1,648,617.54**
PAYDAY #1	PAYDAY #2	PAYDAY #3	TOTAL. ALL

REAL ESTATE ON YOUR TERMS
Secrets to profiting $75,000+ per deal by creating
3 paydays... WITHOUT using your own cash or credit

SMART
Real Estate
COACH

Here is a chart giving you a 12 month look back of what we have created for Paydays #1, 2, and 3. Think about the power of these numbers. Literally with $10 down per deal, we've created Payday #2's netting over $6,000. What would you need in the bank to produce that passively to you? Well, using the $6,000 figure, that's $72,000 per year. Using a 5% return on investment, you'd need $1.4 million in the bank, if my math is correct. We used $10 per property. I think that's a cool end result. You can create the same.

Before I outline how they get some equity out, let me say that we try to get it for what they owe. So, the key question is will you sell it for what you owe? If they say yes, you can structure the basic lease purchase by paying their exact payment (we are currently paying on approximately 50 mortgages like this) provided you know that you can get some spread above that amount and that it is marketable. It's not a discussion for this book, but the alternative to that is just taking the deed subject to their existing mortgage so you own it and fully control it.

As stated earlier, but worth emphasizing again – we've actually combined these strategies as well. As a review, here's how that works:

You start out with a lease purchase and, over time, the seller gains confidence in your ability to pay their mortgage monthly; you then call and ask if you can just prepare a deed for them to sign and get notarized. We did that on six or more deals this year so far and intend to do it a few more times. Before you do the Subject To, you want to make sure the seller is clear that the loan stays in their name. We have a custom Purchase and Sales Agreement that we use for these that our attorney has revised over time and there's no ambiguity once they sign it. This is very, very important. Module 11 in the **QLS Home Study Program** has all of our forms and agreements and they're updated there as we revise them.

The last bucket is the over-leveraged home. Think about the market for these as there are still so many sellers in this bucket who think they're stuck and you have a solution.

Over leveraged, remember, are houses where the seller owes more than it's worth. We've done many of these and the key to these is getting a long term lease/purchase or taking the deed subject to. A long term to us is 7+ years and the last two we did were 9+. You can even do a deal for the remaining term of the mortgage. Let's use a simple example:

- $220,000 value
- $240,000 mortgage
- $1,700 payment

Depending upon what market you're in, you'll have to determine if there's any spread possible on that $1,700 payment. But, in my market with a $220,000 value, I couldn't squeeze a spread of $300+ on that and that is typically my minimum. What can you do with this one? Simply find them a buyer and assign it back to them and collect a juicy assignment fee.

On the other hand, I'm doing one right now which started as a lease purchase, but this coming week we're taking the deed and the two mortgages total $240,000, the value is approximately $220,000, but the payment is only $1,400. I will be able to get $1,700+ for it, so I'm okay staying in the deal and, of course, taking the deed helped my decision. As the owners, we'll control everything, we'll depreciate it, and we'll save on insurance as we use the largest non-owner occupied provider in the country who has great rates.

THE FOLLOW-UP

As I was writing the section about you presenting offers to the sellers in the four different buckets, I kept thinking about follow-up and the importance of it. So, I feel compelled to share it with you here.

Many of our deals come from the follow-up. I wish it was as simple as getting the lead sheet from the VA, booking the appointment, and putting the home under agreement (it sometimes is – but it's the exception, not the rule). You need to know that so many deals come together only after the proper follow-up. We've had sellers call back after a year or two and, most recently, one of our Associates had a seller call back from three full years ago. It pays to stick with this business and not deviate or get distracted by other niches.

Here are some bullet points off the top of my head as I think through the system we use to follow-up:

- **SELLER SAYS "NO" ON PROPERTY INFORMATION SHEET YOU RECEIVED FROM YOUR VA OR ON YOUR OWN.**
  I hear a No as a "no not now" unless the reason is super strong and not going to change no matter what. An example I can think of is a property in an estate with several heirs and there's no way they're going to agree to wait. I had that recently, so I literally threw it away. With estates and heirs like that, I simply ask, "Is this something the family would like to close out and take cash out sooner than later, even if getting less?"

  Alternatively, they could wait and structure a higher cash out with us if the time frame is palatable. Many times the heirs just want the money ASAP, unfortunately. If there is only one person making that decision, it's no different than a regular seller situation.

Lastly, in this "no" category, about ⅓ of those answers on a VA Property Information Sheet converts to a deal eventually. Sometimes it's timing and sometimes they just don't know what they're saying no to when on with the VA for the initial call.

- **SELLER SAYS "YES" ON THE PROPERTY SHEET BUT THE TIMING IS NOT RIGHT NOW.**
  That could be they want to try to sell on their own first (all FSBOs, remember, think they can sell or they would not be a FSBO. So let them try and come back to you) and use you as a backup and to that I say to them, "Look, I understand if you can sell tomorrow for cash, that's your best option – but if you don't, use us as a backup (or I'll say "as a Plan B")." I then email them our document about how lease purchase and TERMS work, the advantages of our business, and I stick it in for a 30 day follow-up, unless they told me when to follow-up.

  Don't be afraid to simply ask, "How long are you planning on trying it for before switching directions?" or "Is there a time frame you need to have it sold by?" Just ask and you'll get proper direction.

- **SELLER SAYS "YES" AND THEY'RE MOTIVATED NOW.**
  These are great and you now want to get in front of them for a viewing to use the walkthrough sheet in the QLS Home Study Program. After you leave the house, have built some rapport, and know more details - now you can get the offer constructed and get that over to them.

- **SELLER SAID "YES" OR "NO" ON THE PROPERTY SHEET, BUT HAS NOT RETURNED A CALL.**
  I don't do more than 2-3 messages (depending on how motivated I am to get the deal and what the initial motivation/reason for selling is on the sheet) without a return call. So, if I or someone on my team leaves 2-3

messages without a response, they get a letter in the mail that basically says, "You spoke with us/our VA back on [date of reference] and we have not heard back from you, so call us if you'd like to discuss us purchasing your home."

We have 10 or so of what we call "form letters" prewritten and used for things like:
- o   VA Lead - no answer
- o   Listed with real estate agent
- o   VA Lead - wants all cash
- o   Expired Listing - no call back
- o   ...and more

These are interesting letters to send and forget about because sometimes we'll get call backs 1, 2 and 3 years later like I mentioned above.

Follow-up is key, but keeping too many junk leads in your files will only bog you down and slow down progress. It can even make you miss some motivated sellers as you get smothered in paperwork. You can listen to some of our Live Seller Calls and follow-up calls in the QLS Modules that will give you a great sample of our scripting.

CREDIBILITY

Unfortunately, in business – any business and any industry – you will always see people who are unethical and out to hurt people. We have seen this over the years in the banking industry and financial planning industry, as well as in real estate. As a result, you will want to make sure you do all you can to put yourself in the right position that screams credibility.

Of course, that starts by you doing the right thing and truly helping people, which is one of the reasons our family team loves doing these transactions. We have each repeatedly said to each other, "It's such a positive business when we can help sellers by purchasing a property they felt stuck with and helping buyers who felt they lost the dream of home ownership." We love the positive energy and you will as well.

We had a buyer once who called on a home of ours. That home already had one applicant in the system with us and, as our custom Deposit Receipt Agreement brilliantly says, we can continue to take applicants and binder deposits until we accept one. At that time, those not accepted of course receive their deposit back.

Here's what happened: that buyer went to view the home and, while there, ran into the person who already applied and put down a $1,000 binder. This person wrongly assumed we were doing something incorrect and collecting deposits or signing leases with multiple people. Of course we didn't, couldn't, and wouldn't – but that was their impression. How did I know this? That second buyer booked an appointment to come to our office, apply, and put down a binder. As I waited for two hours and realized they were a no show, I got a text that basically said something like, "You guys are a scam, you're illegal, and I checked that you're not even registered with the Better Business Bureau."

OUCH! That hurt my ego and my feelings. I wish we could have explained properly, but it was way past that stage. Frankly, it was a big loss for that potential buyer we could have helped, but we always try to turn an experience into a learning lesson. So, out of that experience, we did three things. You can do these exact same things and avoid the scenario I just described:

1. We joined the Better Business Bureau and you'll see that now on our website and social media accounts, we proudly expose the Accredited BBB rating. We applied to get accredited status because anyone can join. We have an A+ rating and actually were asked to do a video on the BBB site, which we did. So many people have commented that one thing on our site was a major deciding factor in dealing with us. Many of our Associates have also achieved Accredited BBB Status and we can assist you as mentioned above.

2. We joined the local chapter of the Chamber of Commerce and posted that on our site and social media accounts.

3. When we meet buyers, we're super clear verbally and in writing while drawing their attention to the wording on the deposit receipt agreement that we are taking other applicants until such time we accept someone. We also encourage them to get resourceful with their deposit because that may push immediate acceptance (typically for a 10% deposit, we'll pull it off the market immediately, so they know they're done and accepted).

LEARN MORE

We have a FREE webinar that you can sign up for right now by visiting: **smartrealestatecoach.com/webinar**

With this book, we've given you a good overview of the Sandwich Lease. The "Real Estate On Your Terms" webinar will give you an introduction into how we're able to do several deals per month with our small family business – not just Sandwich Leases, but Assign Out, Owner Financing, and Subject To deals as well. It will also explain how we create more than 3 Paydays in some circumstances and break down a number of real case studies. You'll also hear from some students via video. The webinar is loaded with some free gifts, including a strategy call with us.

SMART Real Estate COACH

REAL ESTATE ON YOUR TERMS

THE QLS QUANTUM LEAP SYSTEM

Please Note: The earnings of Chris Prefontaine, Smart Real Estate Coach team members, or those of our students and partners are in no way average or guaranteed. Any examples provided in this presentation should not be considered typical, as your results will vary based on many factors.

A PRESENTATION BY THE TEAM AT SMARTREALESTATECOACH.COM

When you buy the QLS Home Study Program, you will also get a 15-minute strategy call with us, as well as one (1) ticket to our annual QLS Live Event in Newport, RI like we mentioned at the beginning of the book.

We'd also appreciate if you took the time to connect with us on any of our web and social media platforms:

- **smartrealestatecoach.com**
- **facebook.com/smartrealestatecoach**
- **youtube.com/smartrealestatecoach**
- **instagram.com/smartrealestatecoach**

Each week on these accounts, you'll find a Deal Structure Sunday, Motivational Monday, and Q&A Thursday video — as well as all kinds of other updates from the team and our Wicked Smart Community. So, be sure to like, follow, subscribe, and share!

RESOURCES

These are all of the links for the general resources that we use. A current and updated list is always available on our website at:
smartrealestatecoach.com/resources

- CREDIT REPAIR: **mycreditteam.com**
  Use our promo code *PREFO*
- VA STAFFING: **reiassistant.com/smartcoach.html**
- APPLY TO BE AN ASSOCIATE: **smartrealestatecoach.com/apply**
- FREE VIDEO LESSONS: **youtube.com/smartrealestatecoach**
- OUR MAIN LEAD SOURCE - MY +PLUS LEADS:
  registration.myplusleads.com/smartcoach
- LIVE ANSWERING SERVICE FOR REAL ESTATE YELLOW LETTERS AND POSTCARD RESPONSES:
  my.patlive.com/signup/PartnerPage.aspx?SOURCE=ANCFPP
- FREE LIVE WEBINAR: **smartrealestatecoach.com/webinar**
- QLS HOME STUDY COURSE: **smartrealestatecoach.com/qls**
- SELLER SPECIALIST PROGRAM: **smartrealestatecoach.com/ssp**
- THE 31-DAY BILLIONAIRE COURSE:
  smartrealestatecoach.com/billionaire

If you would like any of the forms that we describe in this book, just contact **support@smartrealestatecoach.com** and request access.

ABOUT THE TEAM

CHRIS PREFONTAINE
Founder & CEO

Chris Prefontaine is a three-time best-selling author of *Real Estate on Your Terms*, *The New Rules of Real Estate Investing*, and Moneeka Sawyer's *Real Estate Investing for Women*. He's also the Founder and CEO of Smart Real Estate Coach and host of the Smart Real Estate Coach Podcast.

Chris has been in real estate for almost 30 years. His experience ranges from constructing new homes in the '90s and owning a brokerage to running his own investments (commercial & residential) and coaching clients throughout North America.

Today, Chris runs his own buying and selling businesses with his family team and they're in the trenches every single week. They also help their Associates do the exact same thing all across North America, working together on 10-15 properties every month. Having been through several real estate cycles, Chris understands the challenges of this business and helps students navigate the constantly changing real estate waters.

ZACHARY BEACH
COO & Coach

Zachary is an Amazon Best-Selling Author of *The New Rules of Real Estate Investing* and co-host of the Smart Real Estate Coach Podcast. He is a Partner, COO, and Coach at Smart Real Estate Coach. In September 2020, they'll be releasing a revised edition of *Real Estate On Your Terms*, which Zach will be co-authoring.

At the age of 25, Zach decided to leave the world of bartending and personally training and jump into the family business. It was one of the first big risks that he took in his life, as nothing was guaranteed. Plus, he knew absolutely nothing about real estate. Through hard work, in-house training, and implementation, Zachary has completed over 100 deals and growing.

On top of that, he coaches students around the country on how to buy and sell property just like his family still does. Now, as a group, they buy and sell 10-15 properties a month with a predictable and scalable system, controlling between $20-$25 million of real estate at any one time with little to no money in the deal and no banks involved.

Zach has been in the business for over 4 years and runs all operations of Smart Real Estate Coach, while continuing to coach his students. He has an amazing wife Kayla and two small children, his son Remi and his daughter Bellamy. He is a prime example of how to be successful both in business and at home.

NICK PREFONTAINE
Partner & Coach

Nick is part of the Smart Real Estate Coach family, located in Newport, RI. He recently co-authored the best-selling book, *The New Rules of Real Estate Investing*, working alongside his father Chris, his brother-in-law Zach, and a great support team. In September 2020, they'll be releasing a revised edition of *Real Estate On Your Terms*.

Nick grew up in the real estate industry and got started on his own at an early age. Most notably, he was knocking on Pre-Foreclosure doors at age 16, doing up to fifty doors a day. This experience helped shape Nick's real estate career. Now, Nick specializes in working with lease purchasers to get them into a property on the path to home ownership. Regardless of a buyer's credit situation, he looks at their complete financial picture and comes up with a plan to get them into a home.

In 2003, Nick was in a snowboarding accident that left him in a coma for over 3 weeks. The doctors told his parents that he probably wouldn't walk, talk, or eat on his own again. Less than 3 months later, he was running out of Franciscan Children's hospital. Now, in addition to his work in real estate, Nick is a Certified Infinite Possibilities Trainer and speaks to groups that benefit from his message of overcoming adversity.

LAUREN BULK
Director of
Sales & Community

RYAN STAPLES
Director of
Creative Services

VEE HOLLERO
Support
Manager

KRISTEN GALLANT
Executive Assistant

www.ingramcontent.com/pod-product-compliance
Lightning Source LLC
Chambersburg PA
CBHW060530280326
41933CB00014B/3124

9 780578 682068